Cattail

Qui yihahs

Skunk
Cabbage

Balsam
Root

Choanito

Bear
Grass

Chayeyu

Ye'iitsoh

Box
Leaf

Monkey
Flower

Morel

Oregon Reads 2014

Purchased with a grant from the
Jackson County Cultural Coalition
funded by the Oregon Cultural Trust

JACKSON COUNTY
Library Services

Everyone Out Here Knows

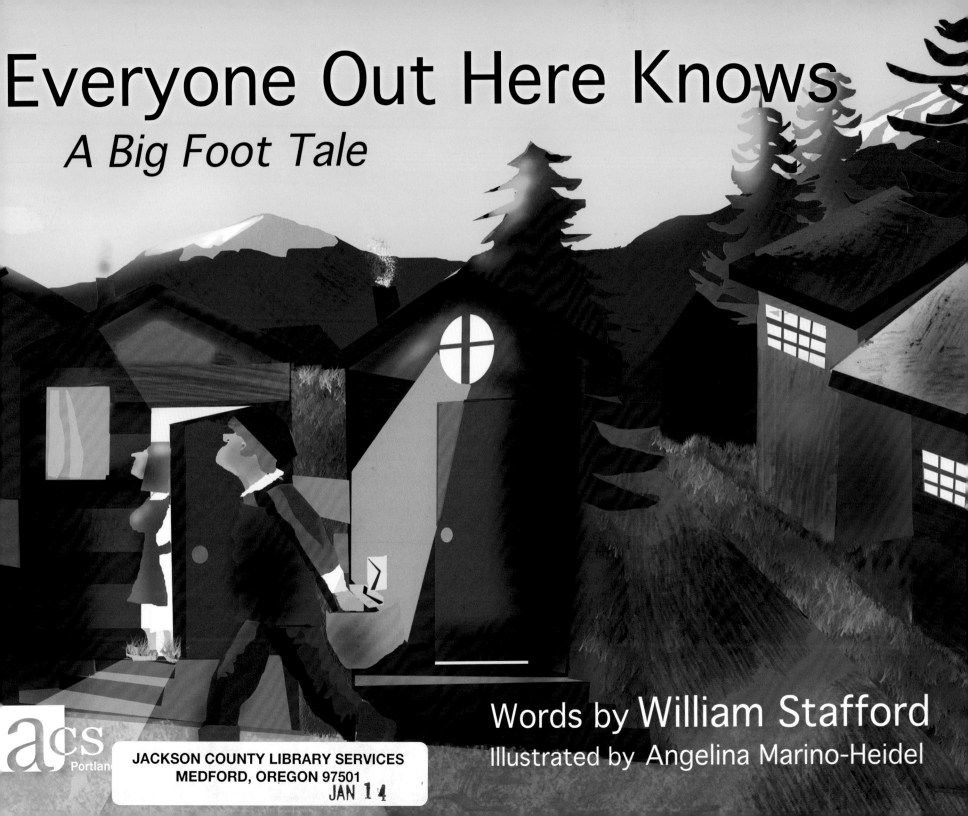

Everyone Out Here Knows

A Big Foot Tale

Words by William Stafford

Illustrated by Angelina Marino-Heidel

To Joel and Ilka
for their love and support

–A. M. & T. B.

Publisher's Cataloging-in-Publication Data
Stafford, William
Everyone Out Here Knows: A Big Foot Tale. —1st ed.
p. cm.
811.5
1. Sasquatch—Poetry. 2. Northwest, Pacific—Folklore. I. Marino-Heidel,
Angelina, ill. II. Title
Stafford, William
Pre-assigned LOC Number 2013912567

ISBN: 978-0-9838168-2-9
© 2014 by Arnica Creative Services
Illustrations © 2014 Angelina Marino-Heidel
Printed in the U.S.A. All rights reserved

Everyone Out Here Knows was previously published in the following Works:
The Long Sigh the Wind Makes: Poems by William Stafford,
ISBN: 0-9629194-0-3 © 1991 by Adrienne Lee Press, poems by William
Stafford, illustrations by Barbara Stafford-Wilson; and in *Starting with Little
Things: A Guide to Writing Poetry in the Classroom* by Ingrid Wendt,
published by the Oregon Arts Foundation © 1983.

Creator and Compiler: Tim Barnes
Illustrations: Angelina Marino-Heidel
Book Cover Design: Angelina Marino-Heidel and Tim Barnes
Interior Design: Angelina Marino-Heidel and Tim Barnes
Project Advisor: Ilka Kuznik
Editor-in-Chief: Gloria Martinez
Design Consultant: Aimee Genter-Gilmore

Introduction

We invite you out to where
the Bigfoot stories grow
and forests go on forever
and mountains get lost in snow.
Where rivers wander into caves
and flowers forget their names.

This is Bigfoot country.
Are the stories true?
Why do we keep hearing them?
There are questions here
and some answers, too.

You will find them
as you follow the trail,
the words and the signs,
of this Bigfoot tale.

—Tim Barnes

Flowers

jump

from the
tracks
of Big Foot

all over
the uplands.

In the
swamp

where turtles
carry their
conservative
houses

Big Foot

waits

disguised

as a shadow.

The mountains are Big Foot's friends.

They

shoulder

around.

They don't want
too much
noise.

They report
any gunshot
into Big Foot's cave

and
mutter
about
it.

Where cliffs are broken,
Big Foot was climbing
with its big hands.

Rivers that swing wide

mysterious places:

you can stand there
and feel the tug
of Big Foot's world.

Everyone Out Here Knows

Flowers jump from the tracks of Big Foot
all over the uplands. In the swamp where
turtles carry their conservative houses
Big Foot waits disguised as a shadow.

The mountains are Big Foot's friends.
They shoulder around. They don't want
too much noise. They report any gunshot
into Big Foot's cave and mutter about it.

Where cliffs are broken, Big Foot was climbing
with its big hands. Rivers that swing wide
are going around mysterious places: you can
stand there and feel the tug of Big Foot's world.

William Stafford

William Stafford, born in Hutchinson, Kansas in 1914, is one of America's most respected and admired poets. His poetry combines accessibility, lyricism, and wisdom. A prolific writer, known for rising early every day to write, Stafford published over four thousand poems and sixty books during a sixty-year career. His second collection of poetry, *Traveling Through the Dark*, won the National Book Award in 1963. In 1998, Graywolf Press published a significant collection of his poetry, *The Way It Is*.

He was the Consultant in Poetry to the Library of Congress in 1970–71, a position now known as the Poet Laureate. In 1974 Governor Tom McCall named him Poet Laureate of Oregon, a post he held until 1989. He died at his home in Lake Oswego in 1993.

After serving four years in public service camps as a conscientious objector during World War II, he became a professor of literature at Lewis & Clark College in Portland, Oregon. Stafford was noted for his generosity, honesty, and for being an enabling presence for self-discovery and growth. The Stafford family (his wife Dorothy and four children) owned a cabin in Sisters, Oregon, in the heart of Bigfoot country, and so Stafford saw for himself the signs that so many have imagined into the myth of Bigfoot.

Compiler's Afterword

I believe in Bigfoot, the idea of him, her or it, because I believe in wilderness, the wild—in rivers, forests, and ravines, in wetlands, meadows and mountains. There's something out there that is huge and hidden, mythic and mysterious. There is something out there that is free to roam.

I discovered "Everyone Out Here Knows" years ago in a book called *Starting with Little Things: A Guide to Writing Poetry in the Classroom*. I was working then as a poet in the Artists-in-Education Program in Oregon. I found myself reading it again and again as I traveled the state doing one-week residencies in schools from Portland to Bend to Ashland. The eyes of the children of Bigfoot country would widen, their imaginations roaming out into the immensities of broad-shouldered mountains and unclimbed cliffs. The delight in those eyes is the beginning of this book.

The poetry of William Stafford found me when I came to Oregon in the early 70s, and it has never let me go. Its lyricism, wisdom, and adventurousness have nourished me. Stafford's poetry is known for its deep sense of place and profound connection to the earth and its enchantments—the mysterious places. This is what animates the poem—an imagination that understands how the wild walks when we wonder.

I've known the work of Angelina Marino-Heidel for many years and saw in her work the style of visual alchemy that could reveal the dimensions of the country where Bigfoot can be imagined, where one thing—a tree, a bend in a river, a body of shadows, a cave mouth, a footprint shining in the rain—can become another thing, a suggestion of immensity and mystery, a projection of possibility, the tug of the wider, wilder world.

—Tim Barnes

About Bigfoot*

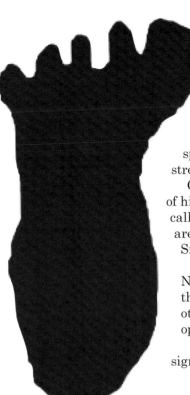

Some people believe in Bigfoot. Some people don't. And some people aren't sure. There are, though, some wide and wild and open spaces out there where the roads don't go, only streams and trees and snow.

Cryptozoology (krip-toe-zoo-all-a-gee) is the study of hidden animals. The people who study Bigfoot are called cryptozoologists. Bigfoot is a cryptid and so are Sasquatches and Yetis and Abominable Snowmen.

Sasquatch is another name for Bigfoot in Northwest country. It's a Native American name that means "Wild Man of the Woods." You can find other Native American names for Bigfoot in the opening and closing pages of this book.

We know hidden animals, cryptids, by the signs they leave, by shadowy likenesses, by mysterious places and sounds, and by the stories people tell after seeing those things and being in those places. What kind of signs of Bigfoot can you find in this book? Have you ever heard a Bigfoot story?

It's up to you to decide whether you think Bigfoot exists or not. If you think he does, what makes you think so? If not, why not? And why is it that people keep talking about Bigfoot?

No one has ever captured one and lived to tell about it, so Bigfoot is a still a big mystery. Mysteries are fascinating things, something to investigate or maybe something to just wander around and wonder about.

—Tim Barnes

*Bigfoot is usually written as one word. Stafford chose to write it as two words for poetic reasons.

Books About Bigfoot and Other Cryptids

For Kids

In Search of Sasquatch, Kelly Milner Halls. Houghton Mifflin Harcourt, 2011.

Looking for Bigfoot (Step into Reading), Bonnie Worth; illustrated by Jim Nelson. Random House, 2010.

Tales of Cryptids: Mysterious Creatures That May or May Not Exist, Kelly Milner Halls, Rick Spears, Roxyanne Young; illustrated by Rick Spears. Millbrook Press, 2006.

For Adults

Anatomy of a Beast: Obsession and Myth on the Trail of Bigfoot, Michael McLeod. University of California Press, 2009.

Bigfoot: The Life and Times of a Legend, Joshua Blu Buhs. University of Chicago Press, 2009.

Giants, Cannibals & Monsters: Bigfoot in Native Culture, Kathy Moskowitz Strain. Hancock House, 2008.

Sasquatch: Legend Meets Science, Jeff Meldrum. Forge Books, 2006.

Where Bigfoot Walks: Crossing the Dark Divide, Robert Michael Pyle. Houghton Mifflin, 1995.

Illustrator's Notes

I thank William Stafford for his vision of the mysterious natural world and the journey his poem took me on. When I was young, my family spent a good deal of time in the forests and mountains of the Pacific Northwest. I'd play freely in the woods from morning until night exploring the things of nature and listening to tales of Bigfoot. My uncle declared that he saw its tracks and my father the Hairy Brother himself. The illustrations in *Everyone Out Here Knows* were inspired by memories of those times. The flora are artistic expressions drawn from wonder rather than botanical exactitude. The flowers depicted generally bloom in the spring. The night sky is based on what Native American tribes called the Full Flower Moon. The constellations of Centaurus and Virgo, although their places in the heavens would be different, appear in spring as well.

In the end papers you will find the names of some of the flora shown in the illustrations. Native American names for Bigfoot can be found in the end papers at the front of the book.

Translations of those names are in the end papers at the back. If you are wandering through the shady ways of the forest, a mountain meadow or high in the uplands, you might just recognize what grows there and know the right name to call Bigfoot if he crosses your path.

—Angelina Marino-Heidel

Look for these in the book

Flora

Arnica
Balsamroot
Bear Grass
Box Leaf
Cattail
Chanterelle
Fiddlehead Ferns
Hedgehog Mushrooms
Jump Up Violas
Monkey Flower
Morel Mushrooms
Skunk Cabbage
Trillium
Wild Mountain Ash
Wood Sorrel

Fauna

Bald Eagle
Dragonfly
Peregrine Falcon
Terrapin
Great Egret
Rainbow Trout
Deer
Elk

Websites and Other Sources

The Bigfoot Field Researchers Organization
www.bfro.net

Bigfoot Encounters
www.bigfootencounters.com

Bigfoot for Kids
www.squidoo.com/bigfoot-for-kids

Bigfoot Information Project
www.bigfootproject.org

Oregon Bigfoot.com
www.oregonbigfoot.com

Bigfoot Country Museum
www.bigfootcountry.net

Tristate Bigfoot
www.tristatebigfoot.com

Kentucky Bigfoot
www.kentuckybigfoot.com

Georgia Bigfoot Society
www.georgiabigfootsociety.com

Bigfoot Lunch Club
www.bigfootlunchclub.com

American Bigfoot Society
www.americanbigfootsociety166.weebly.com

Other Resources:

Friends of William Stafford
www.williamstafford.org

William Stafford: Modern American Poetry
www.english.illinois.edu/maps/poets/s_z/stafford/stafford.htm

William Stafford Archives
www.williamstaffordarchives.org

Acknowledgments:

We thank Ellen Fader for her guidance, Jim Scheppke and Kim Stafford for their support.

To see more of Angelina Marino-Heidel's art, visit www.ArtSpa.us

To read more of Tim Barnes' work, visit tim-barnes.squarespace.com

To order more copies of
Everyone Out Here Knows: A Big Foot Tale:
Arnica Creative Services (ACS, LLC)
13970 SW 72nd Avenue, Portland, Oregon 97223
www.ideasbyacs.com

Arnica Creative books are available at special discounts when purchased for bulk or premiums and sales promotions, as well as for fund-raising or educational use. Special editions or book excerption can also be created for specification.
For details, contact the sales director at: info@ideasbyacs.com
www.facebook.com/ArnicaCreativeServices
www.facebook.com/pages/The-Arnica-Foundation/296892467